I0162738

The Witches of Nakashige

I Talk You Talk Press

Copyright © 2018 I Talk You Talk Press

ISBN: 978-4-907056-97-1

www.italkyoutalk.com

info@italkyoutalk.com

All rights reserved. No part of this publication may be resold, reproduced, stored in retrieval system, copied in any form or by any means, electronic, mechanical, photocopying, recording or otherwise transmitted without the prior written permission from the publisher. You must not circulate this publication in any format, online or otherwise.

This is a work of fiction. Names, characters, businesses, organizations, products, places, events and incidents are either the products of the author's imagination or are used in a fictitious manner. We have no affiliation with any existing companies mentioned in this story. Any resemblance to actual persons, living or dead, existing stories or actual events is purely coincidental.

Although the author and publisher have made every effort to ensure that the contents of this book were correct at press time, the author and publisher do not assume and hereby disclaim any liability to any party for any loss, damage, or disruption caused by errors or omissions, whether such errors or omissions result from negligence, accident, or any other cause.

For more information, see the Copyright Notice on our website.

Image copyright: © Henrik Winther Ander - Fotolia.com #6565636 Standard License.

CONTENTS

I Talk You Talk Press

1. AKIRA GETS A LETTER

Akira Fujihara got home from work. He looked in his mailbox. There was a letter. This was unusual. Akira didn't often get letters. He got bills and advertising brochures, but not letters.

He took the letter upstairs to his apartment. He took off his shoes and raincoat in the entry hall. He went into his small living room, and poured himself some cold tea. He sat down, and looked at the envelope. The post mark was Nakashige-cho.

Akira stared at it. He had an aunt who lived in Nakashige-cho. He hadn't seen her since he was a child. She sent him a New Year card every year, and he sent one to her. But that was all. The envelope was printed. His aunt was more than eighty years old. Would she have a computer and printer?

He opened the letter and read it.

It was about his aunt. It was from a man called Junpei Hara. He wrote:

---*I own a business near your aunt's house. I found out that you are her only relative. Please excuse me for writing to you, but I am very worried about your aunt. She has many problems. I thought you should know.*

She's more than eighty years old and she lives alone. Her house is old, and it needs many repairs. I don't know if your aunt has the money to pay for them.

Recently there was a fire in the house. It was very small, and no one was hurt. But then, a few days later, your aunt fell over in the garden. She hurt her arm and her leg. But she wouldn't go to the hospital.

It seems it is dangerous for her to live alone. I think she must leave her house and go to live in an old people's home. I cannot tell her this. I am not a family member. But I think that you should write to her, or call her, and tell her that this is the best thing to do.

From Junpei Hara---

Akira read the letter again. He was a very kind man, and he was worried.

It seems my aunt is old and sick, he thought. *I am a very bad nephew. I have never been to visit her. Today is Monday. I will take some vacation days next week. I will leave here on Friday or Saturday. I will stay there for one week. That will be enough time to arrange for an old people's home.*

He cooked himself some noodles and ate them. He lived alone, and he was not a good cook.

After dinner, he went to the desk in the corner of the room. He found writing paper and envelopes. He found a small pile of New Year's cards from January.

I'm pleased I didn't throw these away. My aunt's card will have her address on it, he thought.

He wrote a letter to Hara san. He thanked him for telling him about his aunt. Akira wrote that he was a bad nephew. He had not cared for his aunt. But he would do better in future. He would go to Nakashige-cho to visit her. He hoped to arrive on Saturday. If his aunt had another accident or some other trouble, he wanted Hara san to call him immediately. He wrote his telephone number at the top of the letter.

Then he wrote to his aunt. This was a very difficult letter to write. He didn't want to tell his aunt about Hara san's letter. So he wrote:

--- I have been thinking about you. I plan to take a vacation. I'd like to come and visit you this weekend. I hope that will be convenient. I am looking forward to seeing you after so many years. ---

2. AKIRA PLANS A TRIP TO NAKASHIGE-CHO

The next day, Akira told his boss he wanted to take one week's vacation. Akira worked as a clerk in a big office. It was not a very good job, and Akira didn't earn much money. But it was OK. Akira had no wife and no children. He lived a very simple life.

His boss was surprised.

"You always take your vacation in August," he said. "Why do you want to go away now?"

"I didn't take a vacation in August," said Akira. "Do you remember? Many people in the office were sick. You asked me to cancel my vacation and stay here to help."

"Yes," said his boss. "That's true. So I suppose I have to say it's OK."

On Wednesday, Akira got a telephone call. It was Junpei Hara.

"Hara san! What is it? Did my aunt have an accident? Is she ill?"

"No, no. Fujihara san. Your aunt is the same as usual. But I got your letter. You live in Tokyo, and you must be a busy man. I am surprised you plan to come to Nakashige-cho. It's not necessary. If you tell your aunt she must go into an old people's home, I'm sure she will do what you say. I can take care of everything for you. There is a very nice old people's home near here. I called them, and they have a vacancy. I can arrange everything. When your aunt has moved, and is happy in her new home, you could come to visit her. At New Year maybe."

Akira thanked Hara san very much, but he said, "It is my duty to visit my aunt. Since she has many problems now, I must see her as soon as possible. I have made my plans. I will come to see you of course. I must thank you. If you had not written to me, I would not have thought about her, or worried about her."

Hara san said again that it was not necessary. Hara san would do everything. All Akira had to do was persuade his aunt to move out of her house. He could do that by letter or telephone.

Akira did not change his mind. He had made his plans. He would go to Nakashige-cho.

Once he decided to go to visit his aunt, Akira got more and more excited. He had always lived in Tokyo. He had never visited the west of Japan.

It will be very interesting, he thought. *I might be able to take some good photographs.*

Akira was a very good photographer. He spent his weekends walking alone around Tokyo with his camera. He took photographs of everything, but his best ones were the photographs he took of people. Akira liked people, but he was very shy. He found it difficult to talk to people. He never knew what to say. So he didn't have any friends.

Sometimes he won newspaper photography competitions. Once, a publisher wrote to him. The book publisher asked if they could use his photographs in a book about Tokyo life. Akira sent them a lot of photographs. They used almost all of them. But they didn't pay him for them. They gave him ten copies of the book instead. Akira knew that the publisher had cheated him, but he didn't care. Akira still had the books. He thought maybe his aunt would like one. He put a copy of the book into his suitcase.

Shall I take another copy as a gift for Hara san? he wondered. *No, I won't. I'll buy him some cookies.*

On Thursday night there was a message on his answer phone. It was from Junpei Hara.

"Call me, and tell me what plane you will take. I will meet you at the airport."

Hara san had given his telephone number.

Akira didn't call back. He wasn't taking the plane. He was taking the overnight bus to the city nearest Nakashige-cho. Akira wanted to do things his way. That was a slow and quiet way. He felt that Hara san would tell him what to do. He seemed to be a bossy man.

3. THE PEOPLE OF NAKASHIGE-CHO

Akira slept well on the bus. His back hurt, but he was not so tired. He ate breakfast at the bus station, and took a train to Nakashige-cho. He put his suitcase in a locker at the station. He had the presents for his aunt and Hara san in a small backpack and, of course, his camera.

He walked into the town from the railway station. It was a small place. He saw a neighbourhood map, and found where his aunt's house was. It was in the centre of the town, on a corner. He had not told his aunt what time he would arrive. It was only nine o'clock. *Was that too early to visit someone?* Akira wasn't sure.

He walked to his aunt's house. Opposite the house, there was a hair salon. There was a bench outside. Akira sat down. He looked at his aunt's house. It was very big. It looked strange, because it was the only house in a street of shops. Most of the shops seemed to have apartments upstairs, but this was a normal house, with a fence and a gate and a garden. The shop next door to his aunt's house was a grocery store. Above the door, he could see the name 'Hara'.

So that's Hara san's business, he thought. *It's next door to my aunt's house. I'm sure he knows my aunt very well.*

Akira planned to walk around and look at the town and the people, before he met his aunt. But he felt disappointed. The town was nothing special. So he sat outside the hairdressers for a while.

As he waited, Akira changed his opinion a little. It was Saturday morning. People were walking through the streets. They seemed very friendly. Everyone talked to each other. That was different from Tokyo.

He saw a very tall boy on an extra-large bike racing along the road. The door of the hair salon opened, and an older woman wearing a hat came out.

"Good morning," she said to Akira. "It's a nice day, isn't it?"

"Uh. Oh yes. Very nice," said Akira.

He wasn't used to talking to strangers. The woman smiled at him, and went into the car park next to the salon. She climbed on a tricycle, and rode away very slowly down the middle of the road.

You couldn't do that in Tokyo, thought Akira. *But here, people just smile.*

The people were dressed very casually. Akira saw just one woman who looked like someone from Tokyo. She was also old, but she was very smartly dressed.

Then Akira saw something more unusual. A very small person, dressed in a pink tracksuit, and wearing a purple baseball cap was pushing a shopping cart down the street towards him. It was the kind of shopping cart that very old ladies use. It had a brake, and a seat so you could sit down and rest. The seat opened up to make a box to put shopping in.

It's strange to see such a young person using a cart like that, he thought.

As the person got nearer, Akira was surprised. It was a very old, white-haired woman. She was wearing the clothes of an eleven or twelve year old girl. She stopped next to Akira. He noticed that her eyes were very bright. She looked very cheerful.

The old women crossed the road and went into Akira's aunt's house.

Is that my aunt? he wondered. *She looks very well. She doesn't look like a person with health problems or mind problems. Of course her clothes are unusual. If it is my aunt, maybe her clothes are a sign that she is ill.*

He sat on the bench for a while longer. Then he decided he should go to his aunt's house.

He rang the doorbell and waited. There was no reply. He knocked and shouted – nothing. He pushed the door. It was unlocked. The shopping cart was inside the door. Next to it was a pair of small running shoes. They were pink and had a picture of Minnie Mouse on them. He also saw a pair of black ladies shoes.

Akira shouted again. No one came. He didn't want to walk in – he was from Tokyo. In Tokyo you don't walk into people's houses without being invited. You wait for the person to come to the door and say 'come in'. He listened. He thought he could hear music. A

radio? A television? After a few minutes he gave up.
I'll go and talk to Hara san, he thought.

4. MORE BAD NEWS FROM HARA SAN

Akira went into the store. A man came to the counter.

"Can I help you?" he asked.

"Are you Junpei Hara? I'm Akira Fujihara."

"Fujihara san! Welcome to Nakashige-cho. Have you talked to your aunt yet?"

"I went to the house. There was someone there, but no one answered the door. I knocked and shouted, but no one came."

Hara san smiled sadly.

"Well, you see how it is. The old lady, your aunt, is very confused and forgetful. I worry that she will have a serious accident. How can we help her if she won't talk to us? Come upstairs. We can have a drink and talk."

Hara san called out. His wife came into the shop.

"Fujihara san and I are going upstairs. Look after the shop until I come back."

Hara san and Akira went to the apartment on the second floor. Hara san gave Akira some tea.

"I didn't tell you everything in the letter. But now you are here, I will tell you everything I know."

"Please do, Hara san," answered Akira.

"Well, old people become forgetful. I know that. But I think your aunt is in danger. About two weeks ago, I went to your aunt's house. I took her some vegetables. The door was open, but she was not there. I smelt burning. I went to the kitchen. There was a pot of vegetables on the stove. It was red hot. Your aunt had started to cook something. Then she forgot about it, and went out. It made a small fire. Luckily, I got there before the house burned down. The next time she went out, the same thing happened. This time it was a rice cooker full of rice, but there was no water.

"Then two days later, at night, she fell over in the garden. Luckily, I was out on the street. I called an ambulance. When the ambulance came, your aunt would not get into it. She was very angry. She said she was OK, and she didn't need to go to the hospital. She was angry with me!

"There have been other events too. This week her mailbox was full of fish. I think she got confused. She thought she would put the fish in the refrigerator, but she put it in the mailbox instead. When I spoke to her, she said she didn't buy any fish. She said someone must have played a trick on her.

"Then she ordered sushi. The deliveryman brought it to the door. She told him she hadn't ordered sushi. I had to pay the deliveryman for the sushi. You see how it is. Her mind is going."

"Hara san. You have had a lot of trouble. I am very sorry. Let me pay you for the sushi." Akira took out his wallet.

"No, no. I won't let you pay. My wife and I ate it. It was very good."

Akira bowed. "You are very kind."

"Now, about the old people's home. I have told them your aunt will go there. They are waiting for her. But your aunt must agree to go. Or you will have to find a doctor who will say that her mind is going. That she is not safe. The local doctor won't do it. He is an old friend of your aunt's. He will say she is OK. I have a cousin who is a doctor in the next town. I could ask him to come. Shall I ask him to come today?"

"No. Thank you, but no. I must speak to my aunt first."

"But you tried. She wouldn't come to the door! What else can you do?"

Akira didn't know why he had such a strong feeling, but he thought that Hara san was hurrying him. Akira liked to do things slowly and carefully.

"Please wait. I will try to talk to my aunt again. Thank you for the tea."

Akira stood up. He knew that he was being rude, but he wanted to get out of Hara san's apartment.

He ran down the stairs, through the shop and out onto the street.

He went across the street and sat on the seat outside the hairdressers. He was still holding the box of cookies he had brought as a present for Hara san.

I am very stupid, he thought. *Hara san is worried because he thinks my aunt will burn her house down. Of course, Hara san's shop and apartment might burn too. I should go back and apologise.*

5. A VERY UNUSUAL PERSON

Akira sat and tried to find enough courage to go back to Hara san's store. Then he saw the woman in the pink track suit and purple baseball cap come out of his aunt's house. She was pushing the cart. He jumped up and crossed the street.

"Excuse me. Are you Setsu Fujihara?"

The little woman looked up at him. "No. I'm not. I'm Saito. Mameko Saito. Why do you ask?"

"I'm Akira Fujihara. Setsu Fujihara is my aunt. I came to visit her. But she didn't answer the door. Is she in her house now?"

The little old lady stared at him. She looked very tough. "Did you tell your aunt you were coming?"

"Yes. I sent a letter."

"Why have you come?"

"I was worried about her. I thought I should come and see her. I am her only relative."

"And why did you decide to come now? I have never seen you in Nakashige-cho before."

Akira was sweating. This woman was very small, very old, and wearing crazy clothes, but she was asking questions like a policeman.

"No, Saito san, that is true. I have never been here. I have not seen my aunt since I was a small boy. That's why I don't know what she looks like."

"Well, she doesn't look like me." Saito san took out a mobile phone and looked at it.

"It's eleven o'clock. I will be late. Something is happening here. I don't know what it is, but I don't like it. Don't go to visit your aunt now. Go back towards the railway station. Opposite the bank, there's a bar. It's called Botan. Go in there and wait. Someone will come later."

Saito san walked away, pushing her cart. She walked very quickly.

Akira was puzzled. *What shall I do? Hara san is a normal man. Should I go back and follow his plan? Or should I listen to this crazy woman?*

Akira walked back towards the railway station and went into the bar called Botan. It was empty, apart from a teenage boy sweeping the floor.

"The bar is not open," said the boy.

"I know. But can I wait here please?" asked Akira.

"I can make you a coffee, if you want one."

"Yes, please," said Akira.

The boy made him a coffee. He brought it to Akira. He was very friendly, but Akira didn't want to talk. After a while, the boy went away, and Akira was alone. He could hear the boy in the back room. He seemed to be moving boxes. He was singing.

This place is very different from Tokyo, thought Akira. *But I like it.*

After a while, the boy came back. He brought the coffee pot and refilled Akira's cup. Then he brought a bowl of noodles. "I can't cook," he said shyly. "But it's lunchtime. I'm going to eat. So I made some noodles for you too."

Akira was amazed. These people were so kind! He ate the noodles. They were not very good, but he was hungry.

Suddenly Akira heard bangs and crashes outside the bar. A very tall boy came in.

"Sho!" he shouted. "Sho!"

Akira recognized him. It was the boy he had seen before, on the bike.

The boy who worked in the bar came out.

"Keita. What are you doing here?" he asked.

"Chi-obaa," answered Keita. "She wants me to take this guy to Fujihara san's house. She's looking very angry."

Sho looked worried. "Uh. What's wrong?"

"No idea," answered Keita cheerfully. "But you know what she's like. She wants this guy to go to Fujihara san's house. So I'm going to take him. What time do you finish work? You could come too."

Sho smiled. "I finished an hour ago. I only come in to clean on

Saturday mornings when the bar's closed. So yeah, I can come. It's always interesting when Chi-obaa has a plan."

Akira was very puzzled. *Who was Chi-obaa? Who was this boy who wanted to take him to his aunt's house?*

These boys seemed very nice. He liked them. So he would go with them. He didn't know who Chi-obaa was, but maybe it didn't matter.

He stood up. "I will come," he said. "Fujihara san is my aunt. I am worried about her. But first, let me pay you for the coffee and the noodles."

Sho looked surprised. "Pay? The bar is closed. I gave you coffee, because you looked tired and worried. There is nothing to pay."

"What about the noodles?"

Sho looked embarrassed.

Akira understood that the noodles were the boy's lunch. He had given half his lunch to a stranger.

Sho washed the noodle bowls and the coffee cup. Then they walked out of the bar. Sho locked the door.

Keita's bike was leaning against the outside wall. Keita pushed his bike, and Sho and Akira walked alongside. They started walking back into the centre of Nakashige-cho.

6. THE WITCHES OF NAKASHIGE-CHO

After they had walked a few metres, Keita went up a narrow street.
"Come on, we're going this way," he said.

Akira and Sho followed him.

"Why?" asked Sho.

"Chi-obaa said to make sure no one on the main street saw us
going into Fujihara san's house," said Keita.

They walked up to the top of the street and along a road that was
parallel to the main street. Then they turned downhill again. Aunt
Setsu's house was on a corner. The main entrance was on the
shopping street, but there was a small door to the house on the side
street. Keita pushed his bike through the door. It was a kitchen
entrance. He put his bike against the wall. Keita and Sho took off
their shoes and walked into the house. Akira didn't know what to do.
He waited out on the street.

Keita came back. "Come on," he said. "There's a meeting, and
everyone is waiting for you."

*A meeting? Perhaps it's a meeting to decide my aunt's future. But why are
these teenage boys there? Are they some relatives I don't know about?* wondered
Akira.

Akira followed the tall boy. They went through the kitchen, and
into a hallway. The sliding doors to a large room were open. It was a
beautiful room. Through the windows of the room, Akira could see a
traditional Japanese garden.

Hara san had written that the house was old and needed many
repairs.

14

It's old. But it seems to be in good condition, thought Akira.

There were a number of people in the room. Akira stared. There was the crazy old lady in the pink track suit. There was the lady from the hair salon, who rode the tricycle, and the very smartly dressed woman he had seen that morning. Another woman was kneeling at a low table. He had not seen her before. She was pouring tea. The boy, Sho, was kneeling next to her.

That must be my aunt, he thought.

He bowed. "Excuse me," he said. "I am Akira Fujihara…"

"Sit down and drink some tea!" Saito san sounded impatient.

Akira sat down. Keita sat down next to him, and patted him on the back.

"Relax!" he said. "The witches of Nakashige-cho are here. You are quite safe!"

Akira was shocked. There was Saito san of course. Maybe she was crazy. But the other women were very normal old women. He thought Keita was very rude to call them witches.

He looked around the room.

"Keita! Keita!" said the beautifully dressed woman. "You are a very rude boy!" But she was smiling.

Sho took the teacups and gave one to everyone. Akira stared at his aunt. She seemed very normal.

"Aunt Setsu. I am Akira. I have never visited you. I am sorry. But I heard you have problems. I want to help."

"Oh, your aunt has problems," said Saito san. "But the problems are bigger than you think."

"Slow down," said the smartly dressed woman. "The poor man doesn't know anything. He doesn't know who we are."

She smiled at Akira. "Did you come from Tokyo today?"

"No. I left Tokyo last night. I took the overnight bus."

"You must be tired. And now you have all these strange people to deal with. I'm Hanae Yamamoto. I lived in Tokyo for many years, but I came back here to my home town."

I was right! thought Akira. *She has the Tokyo style.*

"I'm Hatsuko Nakamura," the tricycle lady said. She was still wearing her hat. "You've met the boys. Did they introduce themselves properly?"

"Uh." Akira didn't know what to say.

"Of course they didn't. The nice quiet boy is Sho Wada, and the cheeky one is Keita Sato."

Both boys smiled at Akira.

"And me of course," his aunt spoke for the first time. "It's wonderful to see you. The last time I saw you, you were about ten years old."

"Yes Aunt Setsu. And I feel very bad about that. I haven't been a good nephew to you…"

"Enough about that. I have things to do this afternoon, and we need to have a meeting first. We must make a plan." Saito san sounded angry.

"But I thought someone called Chi-obaa wanted to see me. Are we waiting for her?" asked Akira.

"That's Chi-obaa," said Keita pointing at Saito san. "No one ever calls her by her proper name."

"Now can we start?" asked Chi-obaa. "As I said, I have a lot to do this afternoon. I have an hour before my ukulele concert."

"Did she say ukulele concert?" Akira whispered to Keita.

"Probably," Keita whispered back. "It's one of her hobbies."

"Be quiet Keita! Now, Fujihara san. Why did you come here? Do you need money? Did you think your aunt was rich?"

"No, no!" Akira was very upset. He looked at his aunt. "I got a letter. It said that you were sick. That you had an accident. That these days you have some problems. I felt very bad about it. I took some vacation from work, and came as soon as I could."

The four old ladies looked at each other. There was silence. Then Setsu asked, "Who was the letter from?"

"Your neighbour, Hara san."

The women all started talking to each other at once.

"I knew it!"

"That man is a rat!"

"Can you believe it?"

"I told you it was him!"

Then Chi-obaa spoke to Akira. "Did Hara san suggest a plan?"

Akira was sweating again. This tiny woman made him nervous.

"Uh. He said that Aunt Setsu was in danger. That something bad might happen to her. A serious accident."

He looked at his aunt. "He said you would be safer in a home for old people."

"Did he suggest a suitable old people's home?" Hanae spoke

16

quietly, but Akira thought she was very angry. All the women looked angry.

"Yes. He said he had found a place for you, Aunt Setsu. It's very near here. He said it was very nice."

"Did he tell you that the old people's home belongs to his brother?" Hanae asked.

"No. He didn't."

Aunt Setsu nodded to Sho. He took the teapot and went around to refill the cups.

"And did he tell you about all the events that have happened in this house?" she asked.

"He told me about the pot and the rice cooker. Your fall. The sushi order, and the fish in the mailbox," said Akira.

"Yes. Well, he was telling the truth. All those things happened," said Aunt Setsu.

Chi-obaa had been quiet. Now she spoke.

"We're having this meeting to talk about what to do about it. The first thing is that your aunt is not losing her mind. Those things all happened when she was out of the house. When she wasn't at home. Someone arranged all those events. Someone is trying to make trouble for your aunt."

"Why?" Akira couldn't believe it.

"We think the reason is because..." Hatsuko started to explain.

"Not now, Hatsuko. I'm in a hurry. You can tell him later. I have a plan. So please listen."

Chi-obaa started talking. After five minutes, everyone was nodding. It seemed to be a good plan. Akira had some extra ideas. He suggested them. Chi-obaa said his ideas were excellent. Then she got up.

"I have to go now. You all know what you have to do. I'll see you later."

Sho and Keita followed Chi-obaa out of the room. They were going home to tell their parents that they planned to study together until late. Sho would tell his parents he was studying at Keita's house and staying the night. Keita would tell his parents he was going to Sho's house.

After Chi-obaa and the boys left, the room seemed very quiet.

Hatsuko and Hanae looked at each other. "We have a lot to do before tonight, so we will go now," said Hanae.

"We are very pleased you came to see your aunt," smiled Hatsuko. They left. Akira's aunt was still sitting next to the teapot.

"You look a lot like your father," she said.

"So do you," said Akira. "When I look at you, I see my father."

"I wish you had told me you were coming," said his aunt. "I would have prepared for your visit."

"But I did! I wrote you a letter."

"Maybe it arrived the day the fish was in the mail box. There was an envelope, but I threw it away with the fish."

"Aunt Setsu. Can you explain what's happening?"

"You know what's been happening. And Chi-obaa explained. We have to find out who is doing these terrible things to me. Of course, she is sure it is Hara san. But we have no proof."

"Hara san! Why?"

"Hara san wants to open a supermarket. He needs more land. He wants me to sell him this house. I don't want to sell it. He asked me almost every day. He got angry when I said no.

"He stopped asking me. But then, these strange things started happening. Every time, it was Hara san who told people about them. No one thought that was strange. He lives next door. Of course, many people think that I am getting old and forgetful. Some people even told me I was very lucky that Hara san was my neighbour."

"I don't think you are getting forgetful."

"I am starting to forget things. But I am not so bad yet. Let's talk about other things."

Setsu asked Akira about his life in Tokyo. He told her about his photographs. He opened his backpack. He took out the book and gave it to his aunt.

She was amazed. "Akira! These are wonderful photographs. You are a professional!"

"No, no. Just an amateur." But Akira was very pleased that his aunt liked the book.

18

7. A BUSY AFTERNOON

Hatsuko went back to the hair salon and asked Noriko, her daughter-in-law, to do her hair.

"I'm going out," she said.

"But you always wear a hat!" said Noriko. "I can never understand why you always want your hair to be perfect. No one ever sees it."

"But I know what's under the hat." Hatsuko thought this was a perfect explanation.

"OK, but we're busy this afternoon. You'll have to wait."

"That's not a problem. I think I'll just sit here and chat to the customers."

Noriko thought her mother-in-law was behaving strangely. Usually, she didn't talk much. But that afternoon she chatted to everyone.

"I'm going out tonight. Hanae Yamamoto is taking some friends to dinner at a new restaurant. She is going to pay. She has invited me, Chi-obaa, and Setsu Fujihara. Fujihara san has been worried lately. So it was nice of Yamamoto san to invite her too."

"Which restaurant?' asked one of the customers.

"The seafood restaurant that just opened in Hamamura. It's very close to the railway station, so we'll go on the train."

"You're lucky," said another customer. "I heard that it's very good, but very expensive."

"Well. Yamamoto san said she was bored. She wanted to try something different."

Everyone in the salon nodded. Hanae Yamamoto had been born in Nakashige-cho, but she had left the town when she was very young. Many years later she came back. She had beautiful clothes and seemed to be rich. She never said anything about where she had been, or what she had done, but most people thought she had lived in Tokyo. Of course she would get bored in Nakashige-cho.

"What time are you going?" asked Noriko.

"We'll have a reservation for six thirty. That's good for us. We're all old ladies. We'll have a wonderful time and be home by nine thirty."

Noriko found time to do her mother-in-law's hair.

When she finished, Hatsuko looked in the mirror. She nodded. "Very nice," she said. Then she put her hat on and went upstairs to the apartment over the salon.

Nakashige-cho is a very small town. Nothing much happens there, but people like to talk anyway. By 4:00, everyone knew about the ladies' night out.

Hanae Yamamoto had a more difficult afternoon. The restaurant in Hamamura was very popular. It was fully booked. She wanted a table for four people.

"I'm sorry. It's impossible," said the restaurant manager.

Hanae sighed to herself. *Why couldn't Chi-obaa choose something simple? Like going to the movies.*

"Oh. That's a pity. I wanted to bring my friends for a very special occasion. I heard that some very important people eat there. Is that true? Hamamura is a very small town. Do important people really travel to your restaurant to eat?"

"It's true. We are becoming very famous. I shouldn't tell you this, but tonight, Takashi Fujii, who owns the Oki-Fujii sports shop chain, is coming with his family. And the Governor is bringing an important visitor from Tokyo."

"I can understand why I can't get a reservation. But sometimes, busy people have to cancel. If you get a cancellation, will you call me please?" asked Hanae.

"Of course."

Hanae tried calling Chi-obaa. There was no answer. She picked up her jacket and handbag, and went out.

The ukulele concert was in the community centre. Hanae went in. She could hear music. She opened the door to the concert room very gently.

Chi-obaa and the other members of the group were on the stage.

Hanae stood by the door until Chi-obaa saw her. Then she waved. At the end of the piece, the audience clapped, and Chi-obaa left the stage and hurried over to Hanae.

"What do you want? My solo's next!"

"There's a problem with the restaurant. I need some information," said Hanae.

Hanae explained what she wanted, and Chi-obaa told her what she wanted to know.

Satisfied, Hanae walked back to her apartment and made a phone call. Then she made herself a coffee and read a magazine while she waited for the phone to ring.

It was about 30 minutes before the telephone rang. It was the restaurant manager.

He said, "We have had a cancellation. Fujii san has an unexpected meeting. So do you still want to come?"

"I'm so sorry Fujii san and his family can't eat at your restaurant tonight. I guess this often happens to important people. But yes, I would like their table please," said Hanae.

Twenty kilometres away, in the next city, Fujii san was wondering how he could explain to his family that they could not go out tonight. When he was building his company, he had done some things he shouldn't have. Most people didn't know about them. But the woman with the beautiful voice and the Tokyo accent did. Luckily, she didn't want money. She had just asked him to stay at home tonight.

Akira went to see Hara san. This time he remembered to give him the cookies from Tokyo.

"I'm sorry I left so quickly this morning. I think I was tired and confused after my long trip. I'm feeling better now. I am thinking what to do about my aunt," he said.

"The best thing you can do is to ask my cousin, the doctor, to come and see your aunt. He could come tomorrow."

"I don't know. I have been thinking about the accidents you told me about. I was thinking that they could happen to anyone. After all, no one was hurt and there was no real damage. Just a burnt pot and broken rice cooker. I have sometimes forgotten a pot on the stove. Haven't you?" said Akira.

"But what about the fish in the mailbox?"

"Maybe some children were playing a joke," answered Akira. "It wasn't a nice joke. But maybe that's all it was."

"And the sushi?"

"Oh, companies often make mistakes," said Akira. "I don't want to do anything too quickly. Unless something more serious happens, I will wait and see."

"Are you going to stay with your aunt?"

"No. I will go back to the city and find a hotel near the railway station. I'll come back here tomorrow."

Akira left Hara san's store and walked to the railway station. He took a train towards the city. He got off the train at the next station and walked back to Nakashige-cho. He was tired when he got there. He didn't go near the shopping street. He walked along the back streets and came to the narrow side street next to his aunt's house. He went into the house. His aunt was in the kitchen.

"Sho and Keita will be here soon. I've made food for all of you, but make sure you put everything away. We don't want any visitor to realize there are other people in the house. And tell Keita not to talk too loudly. He's a very noisy boy!"

Aunt Setsu left before 6:00pm.

8. WAITING AND WATCHING

Hanae, Hatsuko, Chi-obaa and Setsu caught the 6:00pm train to Hamamura. They were all wearing their best clothes, and looked very excited.

Not long after the ladies left, Sho and Keita arrived. Keita had left his bike at home. They met in a small room next to the kitchen. Aunt Setsu had closed the curtains, so that no one could see in. She also pulled the screens down over the kitchen windows.

"We will have to set everything up before it gets dark," said Akira. "We can't turn any lights on."

He took his camera and a small tripod from his backpack. "My camera takes movies, and I can set it to night-time video," he said.

It took them a long time to find a good place to put the camera. If it was Hara san who came, they thought he would come from behind his store, over the fence, and through the back garden.

"It won't be good enough just to get a photograph of someone in the garden," said Keita. "If it is Hara san, he can say he was coming to the house to check that everything was OK."

Finally, they took everything out of a tall cabinet in the kitchen. It had a glass door, but Aunt Setsu had hung curtains inside so you couldn't see in. There was just enough room inside for Sho, and the camera on its tripod. They taped the curtains around the lens of the camera. They hoped that whoever came wouldn't notice. There was a small gap in the curtains above the camera so that Sho could see out.

Akira showed Sho how to operate the camera.

Keita had brought a camera from his home. Aunt Setsu's house had two floors, but the kitchen was at the back of the house and it was only one storey high. He planned to climb out of an upstairs window and lie on the roof of the kitchen. His job was to watch the back garden.

Akira would wait at the top of the stairs. The lights would be out, and he didn't think anyone would notice him. He was worried about the safety of the two boys. They were very happy and excited, but Akira thought that if anyone saw them, there might be trouble.

When everything was ready, they went back to the little room near the kitchen. They sat on the floor, and ate the food that Aunt Setsu had left for them. They spoke quietly.

"Maybe no one will come," said Akira. "We might be waiting for hours, and there will be no one."

"Oh, someone will come." Keita was cheerful. "Chi-obaa said that if everyone thought the house was empty, the person who has been doing these things would come again. I think it's Hara san. Chi-obaa thinks so too, and she's never wrong."

"But some of the things that happened might have been accidents." Akira was not feeling confident. "My aunt fell over in the garden. No one could make her do that."

"They could." Sho put down the rice ball he was eating and looked at Akira. "The fall in the garden was the one thing Fujihara san wouldn't have done herself."

Akira was confused. "I don't understand."

"There was a rope tied across the garden. It was about thirty centimetres above the ground. It was dark, and Fujihara san didn't see it. She fell over the rope. It was a very mean thing to do. She could have been badly hurt.

"Of course, Hara san thought that she would go to hospital, so he would have a chance to take the rope away. But Fujihara san wouldn't go to the hospital. The next morning she found the rope."

"We don't know it's Hara san who has been doing these things," said Akira.

"It's him. Like I said before, Chi-obaa says it's him, and she is never wrong." Keita took another piece of fish.

"Mmm. I have another question," said Akira.

Keita and Sho looked at Akira.

"Why do you call the old ladies witches?" he asked.

Keita's mouth was full of food. He waved at Sho.

Sho looked embarrassed. "It was me. It's my private name for them. I told Keita, and he thought it was funny. He uses it all the time."

"But why? They don't seem like witches to me," said Akira.

"Well, you know that wizards are very clever, and can do amazing things. But they like to keep their power a secret."

Akira didn't know this. "I suppose so," he said.

Keita swallowed the piece of fish. "Sho's a big Harry Potter fan," he explained.

"Oh, I see." Akira didn't understand, but he wanted to be polite.

"So the old ladies can't be wizards. Wizards are men. So they have to be witches. There are a lot of good witches in the Harry Potter books. They aren't always bad people." Sho looked worried. He was a nice boy. He didn't want Akira to think he said bad things about people.

"Do you think the old ladies can do magic?" asked Akira.

"No, no. Not magic. But they are very clever. If they think something is wrong in this town, they fix it. They always know how to do it. And then later, they never want people to know that it was them who solved the problem. It's a kind of magic. And I think they are powerful," said Sho.

"And you and Keita help them." Akira was interested.

"Only sometimes. Most of the time we don't know what they are doing. But sometimes Chi-obaa wants help."

"You are very kind to help Chi-obaa and the other ladies," said Akira.

Keita and Sho looked at each other.

"We always help them if they ask, because …" started Keita.

Akira saw Sho shake his head at Keita, and Keita stopped talking.

"We have reasons, but we don't talk about them," said Sho.

Akira didn't ask any more questions.

He looked at his watch. "Chi-obaa said to be ready by eight. It's almost that time. We should move into our places."

Keita went upstairs.

Akira and Sho tidied away all the food, and the plates and glasses. Then Akira helped Sho get into the cupboard behind the camera. He arranged the curtains, and closed the glass door. He went upstairs and lay on the floor at the top of the stairs. It was very dark in the old house.

He could hear a clock ticking in the big living room. The old refrigerator in the kitchen made a humming noise. Akira waited.

9. NOW WE KNOW

He did not have to wait very long. There was a very small sound from the back of the house. Akira thought that someone was opening the back door of the house very quietly. He couldn't see anyone, but he could see a small light moving. He thought it was a torch. Then he could hear that someone was walking into the kitchen.

There were quite loud noises. It sounded like something heavy was being moved in the kitchen. Akira could smell heating oil.

The person has turned on a heater! Why? he asked himself.

The torchlight reappeared in the back hallway. The back door opened and closed, and then there was silence.

Shall I go down now? wondered Akira.

Akira jumped. There was someone behind him! He turned around. It was Keita. He had climbed back into the house through the window.

"He's gone. It was Hara san," said Keita. "He's gone back over the fence to his place. What did he do?"

They ran down the stairs together. "I think he turned on a heater," said Akira.

In the kitchen, Sho was banging on the cabinet door. They ran to open the cabinet door, and Sho fell out. The camera fell over. Akira caught it just before it hit the floor.

Sho pushed past them, and pulled a power plug out of the wall. There was a click and the sound of a pump, as the heater shut down. The smell of oil was very strong.

Hara san had put the heater very close to a wall. Then he had put newspapers over the front of the heater. In the short time since he turned the heater on, the paper had already turned brown. Akira grabbed the newspaper and threw it in the sink. He turned the tap on.

"I'm pleased you came quickly," said Sho. He was very pale. "I thought I was going to get trapped in a fire!"

Akira was shocked. "It might have been very dangerous. He could have killed you!"

"Be fair. Hara san didn't know Sho was in the cabinet! He just wanted to make a fire." Keita was smiling. "I got good photographs of him. It was dark, but you can see enough, I think. Is there anything on the video camera?"

The smell of heating oil and burnt paper in the kitchen was very strong, so they went back to the other room.

Akira and the boys looked at the video. It was wonderful. It showed Hara san's face clearly. It showed him moving the heater, arranging the newspapers over the heater, and then turning it on.

They opened the windows to get the smell out of the kitchen. They had just finished tidying up the mess, and putting everything back in the cabinet when Aunt Setsu came back. The other ladies were with her. She was carrying a box. It contained a huge chocolate cake.

"Hanae bought this cake for you. She thought you might be hungry."

Aunt Setsu made coffee, and they all went to the formal living room and sat down.

"Did you have a nice meal?" asked Keita politely.

"It was wonderful, thank you," answered Aunt Setsu. "But everything here is very quiet. So nothing happened?"

"Nothing special," answered Keita.

The ladies all looked very disappointed.

"Oh well, it was a good idea, Chi-obaa," said Hatsuko. "Maybe we have to try another night."

Chi-obaa was looking at Akira, Sho and Keita. "No, I don't think so. Keita is trying to tease us. As usual."

"Tell us what happened," demanded Aunt Setsu.

Akira explained everything. He showed them the video on the camera, and Keita showed them the photographs he had taken from the kitchen roof.

"Sho! Are you OK? It was so dangerous!" said Hatsuko

Everyone except Chi-obaa was very worried about him.

"He's fine," said Chi-obaa. "Sho's a strong boy. Now we have to decide what to do. Fujihara san, can you show me how to operate your camera?"

Akira showed her how to work it. Then Chi-obaa took his camera and Keita's camera and put them in her handbag. "I'll give them back to you tomorrow. Now I have to go. It's past ten o'clock, and I don't want to miss the wrestling on TV."

Everyone got up to leave. Akira went with Hanae, Hatsuko and Chi-obaa. He was going to the railway station to get his suitcase. Keita and Sho were staying the night in his aunt's house, and she had asked Akira to stay too.

As he walked out of the room he heard Keita say, "Fujihara san. Is nobody going to eat this chocolate cake? I have to tell you that I'm very hungry."

Walking back from the railway station Akira was very happy. He thought about his life in Tokyo. In Tokyo he never knew what to say to people. His life was very quiet, and sometimes he was lonely. Here in Nakashige-cho he talked to people easily. *I like it here. I would like to stay. These are my kind of people,* he thought.

10. A KIND OF MAGIC

The next morning, Chi-obaa went to visit Hara san. She went very early. The streets were empty. No one saw her.

Hara san's wife opened the door to the shop. She was cleaning before the shop opened. Chi-obaa went in. She went upstairs. Hara san was eating breakfast. Chi-obaa opened her bag and took out the cameras. She showed Hara san the video and photographs. She talked. Hara san tried to talk back, but Chi-obaa wouldn't let him speak.

Then she left. Hara san's grocery store didn't open that day. The next week everything was emptied out of the store. Hara san and his wife went to work for his brother who owned the old people's home.

Hanae Yamamoto went to see the bank manager and her lawyer. She told them both she had a plan.

They both said the same thing to her. "Yamamoto san! Why do you want to buy a shop?"

"Maybe I want to sell hats," she said. "I like hats."

Neither of the men believed her, but they didn't say anything.

A few weeks later, everyone in the hair salon was talking about the latest news.

A famous photographer from Tokyo had decided to live in Nakashige-cho. He planned to open a studio! His studio would be in the building where Hara san's store used to be.

The bank manager's wife was having her hair coloured. She knew who owned the building now. Of course she couldn't say anything, but she thought to herself, Hanae Yamamoto's a clever businesswoman. If she is going to rent her building to this photographer, he must be good. I'll tell everyone to go to him for family portraits.

So everything worked out very well. Everyone was happy, except perhaps for Hara san. But as Chi-obaa said, "Hara san is lucky. He has to work hard as a cleaner at the old people's home, but he might have gone to prison. Life is not perfect. We do our best, but sometimes we can't fix everything."

Sho Wada is very young, but he also knows that life is not perfect. But there are some days when he thinks that life in Nakashige-cho is almost perfect. That's enough. He believes it's a kind of magic. Akira Fujihara, the owner of a successful photography studio and a very happy man, would agree with him.

THANK YOU

Thank you for reading The Witches of Nakashige. (Word count: 8,840) We hope you enjoyed it. We have two more graded readers with stories from Nakashige-cho:
Chi-obaa and Friends
Chi-obaa and Her Town

If you would like to read more graded readers, please visit our website
http://www.italkyoutalk.com

Other Level 4 graded readers include
Chi-obaa and Friends
Chi-obaa and Her Town
End House (Old Secrets – Modern Mysteries Book 2)
On the Run (Old Secrets – Modern Mysteries Book 3)
The Blue Lace Curtain (Old Secrets – Modern Mysteries Book 1)
The Legacy
Vanished Away

ABOUT THE AUTHOR

I Talk You Talk Press is a Japan-based publisher of language textbooks, graded readers and language learning/teaching resources.

Our team is made up of highly experienced language teachers and translators, who have all studied at least one additional language to an advanced level.

This experience enables us to design our materials from the perspective of both the teacher and the learner. We consult with both teachers and language learners when designing our textbooks and graded readers, and test our materials extensively in the classroom before publication.

We are a fast-growing press, and currently publish graded readers for learners of English. We publish new graded readers monthly.

www.ingramcontent.com/pod-product-compliance
Lightning Source LLC
Chambersburg PA
CBHW022349040426
42449CB00006B/798

* 9 7 8 4 9 0 7 0 5 6 9 7 1 *